Amazing Armies

Children's Military & War History Books

BABY PROFESSOR
EDUCATION KIDS

What is an army?

An army is an organized group of people who are trained and equipped to fight, often for the defense of their lands and people and sometimes to take over other countries.

Among all the types of military power, the armies are the most important because people live on land.

Throughout history, land armies guarded the existing territories, and were essential when a country wanted to conquer and control more land.

Let's get to know
the Six Most
Powerful Armies
of All Time.

Rome conquered the western world. They were known to have the ability to fight again and again until they were all defeated.

They were so determined to fight because (1) for a poor soldier, he was promised to own a land after they win the war; (2) for those who already owned lands, it meant protecting what they had and acquiring more riches; and (3) as a whole, victory meant keeping Rome strong and secure.

Over about three hundred years, Rome expanded from just being an Italian power to controlling the land around the entire Mediterranean Sea.

The Mongols started their conquests in 1206 and conquered most of Asia and some of Europe in little more than a hundred years. They were an unstoppable force that dominated Russia, China, and the Middle East.

They owed their success to the various tactics and strategies developed by Genghis Khan, who was the first emperor of the Mongol Empire. They were known for their mobility and endurance.

They broke the morale of their opponents by inflicting major damage and casualties and spreading terror.

The Ottoman Empire conquered most of the Balkans, North Africa, and the Middle East in its heyday. In 1453, they conquered Constantinople, the most impenetrable city in the world. They managed to hold the main part of their land for five hundred years.

They used muskets and cannons which gave them decisive advantage as a young empire. One of their major advantages was the use of elite, special infantry units known as Janissaries. These were composed soldiers trained since their youth, and were very effective and loyal.

The German Army in World War II was able to accomplish great feats through the use of their innovative Blitzkrieg concept that utilized new technologies in communications and weaponry, combined with speed, surprise and concentration of forces for efficiency.

Before 1946, this is known as the Red Army. This army was responsible for turning the tide of World War II.

Due to the enormous size of the Soviet Union's landmass, industrial output, and population, they could field a huge army. Although not all units were strong, as a body they could absorb many losses and were considered as a military juggernaut.

The US Army, at a high state of readiness and competence since 1941, is better than any other army in history at deploying massive amounts of military force in an effective, quick manner.

Though not as large as countries like the former Soviet Union, the US fields a highly trained fighting force using superior technology. They also have the greatest naval and air power the world has known.

With the changes and advancements in modern technology, countries from China to India to Israel have formed powerful military forces that have great potential to affect history.

WW2

Well Rassid had a tank called the t34 in WW2.

WW2

In D-day in WW2 there were 3 bunkers but it was not easy almost 150,000 died.

Made in the USA
Coppell, TX
19 November 2019